THE ST FRED ROGERS

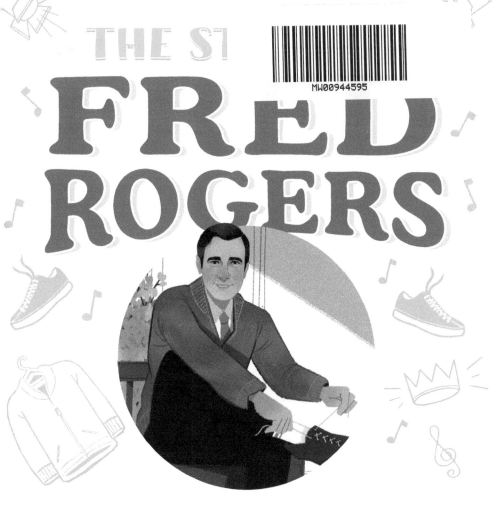

A Biography Book for New Readers

— Written by —
SUSAN B. KATZ

—Illustrated by—
CAN TUĞRUL

ROCKRIDGE
PRESS

To my brother, Steve, who was my very
first friend and still gives me advice
today. We grew up watching Mister
Rogers together and he helped us
believe in ourselves.

For general information on our other products and services or to obtain technical support, please contact our Customer Care Department within the United States at (866) 744-2665, or outside the United States at (510) 253-0500.

Rockridge Press publishes its books in a variety of electronic and print formats. Some content that appears in print may not be available in electronic books, and vice versa.

TRADEMARKS: Rockridge Press and the Rockridge Press logo are trademarks or registered trademarks of Callisto Media Inc. and/or its affiliates, in the United States and other countries, and may not be used without written permission. All other trademarks are the property of their respective owners. Rockridge Press is not associated with any product or vendor mentioned in this book.

Series Designer: Angela Navarra
Interior and Cover Designer: Jane Archer
Art Producer: Hannah Dickerson
Editors: Orli Zuravicky and Eliza Kirby
Production Editor: Jenna Dutton
Illustrations © 2020 Can Tuğrul. Maps © Mio Buono/Creative Market, pp. 2, 16, 24, 30, 40.

Photography © PictureLux/The Hollywood Archive/Alamy Stock Photo, p. 46;
H. Mark Weidman Photography/Alamy Stock Photo, p. 47;
Entertainment Pictures/Alamy Stock Photo, p. 49. Author photo courtesy of Jeanne Marquis.

ISBN: Print 978-1-64739-788-3 | eBook 978-1-64739-473-8

R0

⇒ CONTENTS ⇐

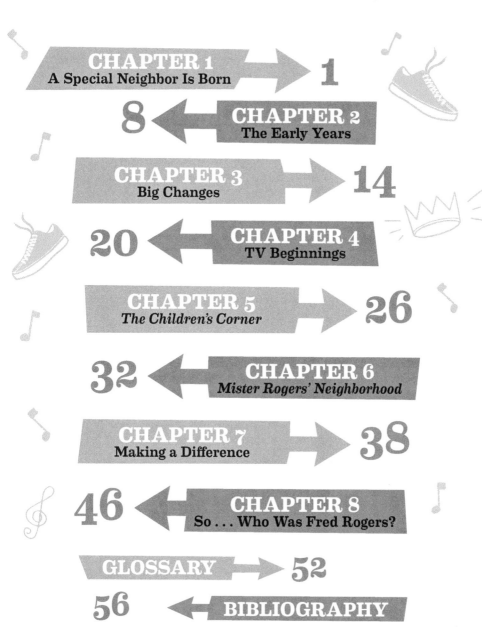

CHAPTER 1

A SPECIAL NEIGHBOR IS BORN

Meet Fred Rogers

Fred Rogers was born with a love of make-believe. He especially loved **puppetry**. Almost every day of elementary school, he put on puppet shows at lunch for his friend Peggy. Fred had a natural talent for making funny voices and telling engaging stories. His shows kept her entertained every time. Peggy was seeing the beginnings of what would become Fred's world-famous children's TV show, *Mister Rogers' Neighborhood.*

Fred grew up in a tight-knit family and **community**. His grandfather, Fred McFeely, was a big part of Fred's life. He helped

Fred build **confidence** in himself and learn to take risks. Grandpa McFeely, or Ding-Dong as Fred called him, was such a big influence that Fred would later name a **character** on the show after him!

Fred wanted kids to have kind, loving people in their lives—just like he had. So he created a brand-new neighborhood in his TV show where he hoped kids would feel just as confident and loved as he felt. Fred also starred in the TV

WHERE?

PENNSYLVANIA

LATROBE

program as himself. Through *Mister Rogers' Neighborhood,* Fred talked about many important subjects in a way that kids could understand. He

> The **real** issue in life is not how many blessings we have, but what **we do** with our blessings. Some people have many blessings and hoard them. Some people have few and **give everything** away.

reached millions of children through his show and made them feel special and important. His kindness made them trust him and listen closely. From 1968 to 2001, Fred Rogers taught children about all sorts of serious and silly things. Let's find out how Fred Rogers helped shape the way millions of children feel about themselves and view the world around them.

Fred's America

Fred McFeely Rogers was born in an old, brick home on March 20, 1928, in Latrobe, Pennsylvania. His parents, Nancy and Jim, welcomed him happily. His grandparents, Fred and Nancy Kennedy McFeely, and the family dog, Ronnie, were also there to greet him. Fred's family was quite **wealthy**. They even had a driver and a chef!

Many people around them were not as lucky. In 1929, the US **economy**—the way people made money and sold goods and services—crashed. That led to the **Great Depression**, a time when much of the country could not find work. People had to line up for hours just to get a loaf of bread and a bowl of soup. Fred's father owned and ran two large factories in Latrobe. The Rogers family was **generous**. At Thanksgiving, they gave out turkeys to their employees.

When Fred was a child, Black people and white people were not allowed to do many things together. In some states, it was even **illegal** for Black people and white people to swim in the same pools or attend the same schools!

JUMP
-IN THE-
THINK TANK

How would you feel if you had to go to a different school because of your skin color?

5

Laws that required Black people and white people to do things separately were called **segregation**. Fred didn't understand why everyone couldn't do things together. His parents felt the same way. When Fred was three years old, his family's housekeeper, Mrs. Allen, passed away. She and her son, George, were Black. Fred's parents invited George to come live with them. George was 11. He became like a brother to Fred. George loved adventure and inspired Fred to have a sense of adventure as well. This curiosity grew stronger throughout Fred's life.

WHEN?

Fred Rogers is born.	Economy crashes; the Great Depression begins.	The Great Depression ends in March.
1928	**1929**	**1933**

CHAPTER 2

THE EARLY YEARS

Fred's World of Pretend

Fred had awful allergies and asthma as a kid. His parents were always worried he was going to get sick. He spent a lot of time indoors, alone, reading or playing with puppets. In 1938, when Fred was 10, his family decided he should spend the summer with another family whose son, Paul, also had bad asthma. The two families put their money together to buy a new, expensive machine: a window air-conditioning unit.

MYTH & FACT

Fred Rogers didn't play outside because he was a shy boy.

Although Fred was shy, he actually couldn't play outside because he had bad allergies and asthma.

Fred and Paul, who was 16, couldn't go outside with the other kids. Instead, the unit was installed in Paul's room, and the boys had all of their meals in there. They stayed inside day and night. Fred would pass the

> Nothing can replace the influence of **unconditional** love in the life of a child . . . children love to belong, they long to belong.

time using his imagination and playing with puppets. Paul was like another big brother to Fred that summer. The following year, Fred's parents adopted a baby girl named Laney. Fred was happy to have a baby sister with whom he

could play.

At school, kids teased Fred, calling him "Fat Freddy." One time, Fred decided to walk home from school. A group of boys chased him the whole way.

Fred's dad told him to ignore the boys and pretend it didn't bother him, but it did! It upset him that those boys treated him poorly because of his weight and shyness. They didn't take time to find out who he was. To Fred, who a person was on the inside was more important than what they looked like on the outside.

Rogers Family Tree

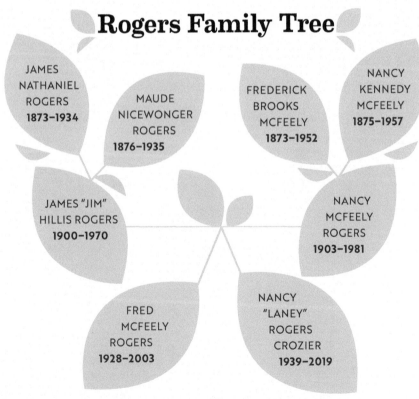

JAMES NATHANIEL ROGERS 1873–1934

MAUDE NICEWONGER ROGERS 1876–1935

FREDERICK BROOKS MCFEELY 1873–1952

NANCY KENNEDY MCFEELY 1875–1957

JAMES "JIM" HILLIS ROGERS 1900–1970

NANCY MCFEELY ROGERS 1903–1981

FRED MCFEELY ROGERS 1928–2003

NANCY "LANEY" ROGERS CROZIER 1939–2019

The Real McFeely

Fred's family was **religious** and went to church
every Sunday. Fred read the Bible from cover to
cover. He also loved to play piano. Whether he
was angry, sad, or happy, Fred could express his
feelings through music! His grandpa, nana, and
mother also encouraged Fred's love of the piano.
They realized that he had an ear for music. He
could hear songs once and then
repeat them. So they
bought him a small
pump piano and, later,
a real piano.

Fred spent a lot of
time on Grandpa
McFeely's farm,
Buttermilk Falls, just
outside of Latrobe. Fred
felt free there. Once, when

Fred climbed up on a stone wall, his mom told him to get down. But Fred's grandpa told her to let him climb. He knew his grandson had to learn to do things for himself. His grandpa believed he could do it, even if he fell down a few times trying. Those days on the farm, Grandpa McFeely would say, "Freddy, you make my day very special just by being you." Fred never forgot those moments with Ding-Dong.

WHEN?

Fred's grandma, Nancy, buys him his first piano.	Fred's sister, Laney, is adopted.
1936	**1939**

CHAPTER 3

BIG CHANGES

An Unlikely Friendship

In high school, Fred did not have many friends, but his mom had an idea that would change his life forever. When the captain of the football team, Jim Stumbaugh, hurt himself during practice, Fred's mom suggested that Fred bring Jim his homework at the hospital. Jim and Fred became fast friends. Fred's unlikely friendship with Jim brought Fred out of his shell. He became more confident and active in school activities. He started swimming a lot and became more fit. Fred also wrote for the school newspaper. He even had a girlfriend—her name was Doris Stewart. In a few short years, Fred went from being a shy kid who spent most of his time alone to being the president of his high school's student council!

> " There are **three** ways to ultimate success. The **first** way is to be kind. The **second** way is to be kind. The **third** way is to be kind. "

By the time Fred graduated from high school in 1946, he was on his way to becoming a star. He was a skilled poet and had won many awards and honors. A strong student and talented **musician**, Fred got into a great college and couldn't wait to see what the future held for him. One thing Fred knew for sure was that he wanted to spend the rest of his life helping people.

Fred's Future

Fred left home in the fall to study at Dartmouth College in Hanover, New Hampshire. Sadly, Fred felt very out of place there. His roommates played football and liked to throw parties.

Fred was more interested in studying. He decided to go back to his first love: piano. He met a music teacher named Arnold Kvam. When Professor Kvam heard Fred's tremendous piano talent, he told him to transfer to Rollins College in Florida because they had a better music program. On spring break in 1948, Fred went to visit Rollins. Professor Kvam asked a group of

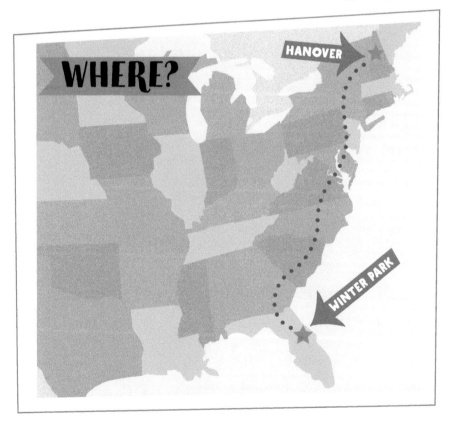

WHERE?

HANOVER

WINTER PARK

students to meet Fred at the airport. One of those students was Joanne Byrd, who became Fred's girlfriend. Fred fit right in at Rollins. The other students were impressed by the jazz and pop tunes Fred played on the piano!

JUMP
—IN THE—
THINK
TANK

Was there ever a time when your plans changed but then worked out for the better?

The next three years were some of the happiest in Fred's life. After graduating from Rollins College with high honors in 1951, Fred planned on becoming a **pastor** at a church. That was, until he came back to visit his parents.

His family had gotten another cool, new machine: a television! Fred thought it was great, but he noticed the kids' shows usually had people in costumes,  throwing pies in each other's faces. He thought that was a silly use of such great **technology**. Fred wanted to use TV to do better things. So, he decided to become a TV star to help kids.

WHEN?

World War II ends.	Fred graduates from high school.	Fred transfers from Dartmouth to Rollins.	Fred graduates from Rollins and decides to work in TV.
1945	**1946**	**1948**	**1951**

CHAPTER 4

TV BEGINNINGS

JUMP
—IN THE—
THINK TANK

Have you ever had a **mentor**, or someone who takes you under their wing and teaches you a skill? How did they help you and what did you learn from them?

 # Off to New York City!

After graduating from college, Fred moved to New York City. He even had his piano delivered to his new apartment. Fred got a job working at the National Broadcasting Company (NBC) as an assistant to a **producer**. He worked for Kirk Browning, who produced and **directed** major programs like *Live from the Met*. Fred mostly got coffee and soda for Kirk. Eventually, Fred became the floor **manager** for Kirk. That meant that Fred would give directions to the **studio crew** and then report back to Kirk. Kirk later said that he was impressed by how much Fred had learned during his time at NBC.

Fred also worked on *The Kate Smith Evening Hour*, where he met famous singers like Maybelle Carter, June Carter, and Hank Williams. He worked on *The Gabby Hayes Show*, one of the first cowboy shows for children. Fred was doing very well, but there was something missing for him. He got into TV to create something of his own for children, not to work on other people's shows.

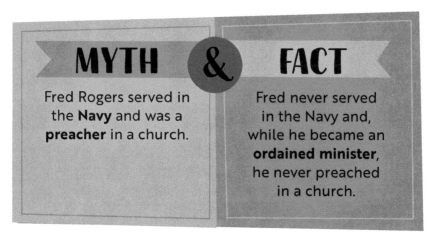

MYTH & FACT

MYTH
Fred Rogers served in the **Navy** and was a **preacher** in a church.

FACT
Fred never served in the Navy and, while he became an **ordained minister**, he never preached in a church.

He kept that idea in the back of his mind for years and never stopped dreaming of his goal.

 ## Home Sweet Home

While working at NBC in 1952, Fred found out that his old girlfriend from Rollins College, Joanne Byrd, was now dating someone else. Fred still loved her very much, so he wrote Joanne a letter asking her to marry him. She called him up and said, "Yes!" They were married in July of 1952. Soon after, Joanne moved to New York City. While Fred was at work, Joanne would stay home and practice playing Fred's piano.

Sometimes Joanne helped Fred with his work. Once, when a singer refused to appear on TV, Fred called Joanne. She took the singer home for a cup of tea and a chat. Joanne talked her into going back to do the show!

Soon after, Fred's dad, James (known as Jim) told him about a new **TV station**, WQED,

opening up in Pittsburgh, Pennsylvania. It was going to be **educational**, which meant that Fred might be able to create some children's shows. Finally, he had an opportunity to do what he'd been dreaming about for years! It was a chance he couldn't pass up. So, in 1953, Fred and Joanne moved back home to Pennsylvania, excited to start this new chapter in their lives together.

WHERE?

NEW YORK

PENNSYLVANIA

PITTSBURGH

NEW YORK CITY

WHEN?

1951	1952	1953
Fred starts working at NBC.	Fred and Joanne get married.	Fred and Joanne move back to Pennsylvania.

CHAPTER 5

THE CHILDREN'S CORNER

# It's Showtime

Fred was excited to work at a new station where he could make a show the way he imagined it. He joined WQED in 1954 as the program manager. His boss was Dorothy Daniel. Together, with a team of people, they came up with a show called *The Children's Corner*. A woman named Josie Carey would sing while Fred played the piano. On April 1, 1954, the night before they were going on air, Dorothy gave Fred a striped tiger puppet. Fred named him Daniel Striped Tiger, after Dorothy Daniel. Fred did the voice of Daniel on the first show.

Daniel Striped Tiger would pop out of an old grandfather clock and share a fact about history with children. They also had special guests on the show. Fred filled in any extra time they had with his puppets. Eventually he brought in more characters, like King Friday XIII and X the Owl. Josie started singing and talking to the puppets. She told them when she felt upset and they listened and helped Josie solve her problems. Parents wrote letters saying how much their kids loved *The Children's Corner*. In 1955, the show won a Sylvania Award for best local children's program in the country.

JUMP
—IN THE—
THINK
TANK

Why do you think Mister Rogers wanted control of his show? How do you feel when you get to make big decisions as a leader?

 Family Life

Fred and Joanne's family was growing. They now had two boys. Their first son, James "Jim" Byrd Rogers, was born in 1959. His brother, John, came along in 1961. Fred was still interested in becoming a preacher, so he took religious classes and became an ordained minister. He also took **child development** classes to understand how children learn and grow.

In 1963, the Rogers family moved to Toronto, Canada, so that Fred could produce a show of his own. Fred called the new show *Misterogers*. He still played the piano and did puppetry, but this show was different. For the first time, Mister Rogers came out from behind the puppet stage and talked to the children as himself, not as a puppet.

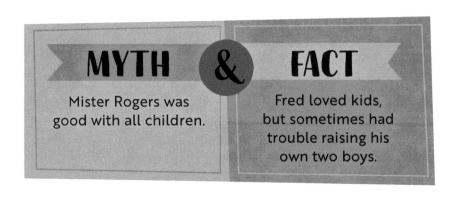

MYTH & FACT

Mister Rogers was good with all children.

Fred loved kids, but sometimes had trouble raising his own two boys.

On *Misterogers*, a trolley took **viewers** to the
Neighborhood of Make-Believe, where Fred's
puppet characters lived. The show taped in black
and white and ran on TV from 1963 to 1967. But
the Rogers family didn't like being so far away
from home and, after a few years in Canada,
they returned to Pittsburgh. Fred went back
to working at WQED, but not on *The Children's
Corner*. Instead, he tried something new.

WHERE?

TORONTO

PENNSYLVANIA

PITTSBURGH

WHEN?

The *Children's Corner* starts.	Fred and Joanne's first son, Jim, is born.	Their second son, John, is born.	Fred's show *Misterogers* debuts in Canada.
1954	**1959**	**1961**	**1963**

CHAPTER 6

MISTER ROGERS'
NEIGHBORHOOD

Fred's Own Show

Fred turned parts of his last show into his new show, *Mister Rogers' Neighborhood.* He added some exciting new things, too. Every show began with Fred entering the door of his "house" while singing a theme song that he wrote and composed. The song was called "Won't You Be My Neighbor?"

Mister Rogers sang while he changed out of his street shoes into blue tennis shoes and then put on a cardigan sweater. Fred's mother, Nancy, knit all of his sweaters by hand. Mister Rogers talked in a slow, calm way that welcomed children to his Neighborhood of Make-Believe, puppetry, and interesting visitors. Mr. McFeely, a character based on Fred's grandpa, delivered the mail. Every time he arrived, he'd say, "Speedy delivery!"

When *Mister Rogers' Neighborhood* first aired in 1966, people loved it! Fred became famous.

Kids would line up with their parents to meet him when he was in public. Until then, most children's shows, like *Howdy Doody* and *Captain Kangaroo*, were silly and funny but did not teach children how to deal with life. Fred offered a very different kind of program. He really connected with the kids watching him on TV.

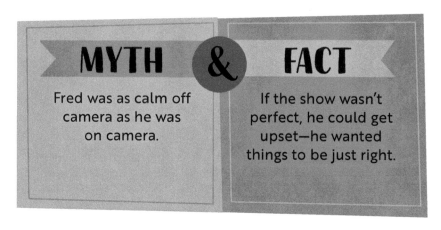

MYTH & FACT

Fred was as calm off camera as he was on camera.

If the show wasn't perfect, he could get upset—he wanted things to be just right.

JUMP
−IN THE−
THINK TANK

Make-Believe and Real

What is it about puppets that makes you feel connected to them? Do you watch and listen to the puppet or look at the person with their hand inside of it?

Puppets like Lady Elaine Fairchilde, X the Owl, and Henrietta Pussycat delighted children everywhere. Fred did the voices for those puppets as well as for King Friday XIII, Queen Sara Saturday, and, of course, Daniel Striped Tiger. He often said that speaking through a puppet was much easier for him—and for the kids listening—than talking as an adult to a child. Fred encouraged children to talk or sing about their feelings, not bury them or feel embarrassed by them. He said, "If it's mentionable, it's manageable," meaning that if you say it out loud, it makes it easier to deal with your feelings.

He often repeated two special sentences that his grandpa McFeely told him as a child: "I like you just the way you are" and "You made today special by just being you."

Fred used the number 143 for the address on his pretend TV house for two reasons. First, he weighed 143 pounds his whole adult life! Fred also realized that the words "I love you" have one letter, four letters, and then three letters, in that order. He thought those were the three most important words in the English language. *Mister Rogers' Neighborhood* was watched by children in

> " When I was a boy I used to think that strong meant having big muscles, great physical power; but, the longer I live, the more I realize that real strength has much more to do with what is not seen. Real strength has to do with helping others. "

almost every home across America for more than three **decades**. At its peak in the 1980s, *Mister Rogers' Neighborhood* reached more than seven million children a day!

Mister Rogers' Neighborhood first airs.

Fred's show hits its peak.

1966 —— **1985**

CHAPTER 7

MAKING A DIFFERENCE

Fred Fights for What's Right

While much of Fred's show was make-believe, Mister Rogers also talked about some very real topics. One day, his goldfish died. Fred talked to the **audience** about death, and told them that it was okay to be sad. He used his television show not only to help kids express themselves, but also to prove that adults will listen to them.

He also wanted to teach kids right from wrong and discuss things that were happening in the world. In 1969, during the **civil rights movement**, Mister Rogers addressed the topic of segregation between Black people and white people in one of his most famous episodes. Officer Clemmons, played by a Black actor named François Clemmons, and Mister Rogers soaked their feet together in a pool. Before the Civil Rights Act of 1964, what Officer Clemmons and Mister

Rogers did was illegal. In 1969, many people still wanted Black and white people to be segregated. Soaking his feet with Officer Clemmons on the show sent a very important message about **equality**.

Mister Rogers' Neighborhood aired on the Public Broadcasting System (PBS), which got money from the government to stay on the air. In 1969,

Congress was considering not giving PBS money to keep shows running. Fred went to Washington, DC, and gave a speech to Congress about why showing kindness to children was important. Fred got PBS the money they needed!

Fred helped kids and parents make sense of very upsetting things and talk about their feelings. He got **advice** from a child **psychologist** named Dr. Margaret McFarland. Mister Rogers used what he'd learned about child development to talk about important events, like the **Space Shuttle *Challenger*** crash and **Martin Luther King Jr.**'s death. In 1981, Fred dedicated a whole week of shows to talking about **divorce**.

Everyone's Favorite Neighbor

Fred Rogers had a huge impact on **generations** of kids. *Mister Rogers' Neighborhood* was on television for more than 30 years! In 1999, Fred was **inducted** into the Television Academy's Hall of Fame. On stage in front of thousands of people, Fred asked everyone to close their eyes for 10 seconds and think of all the people who loved them into being who they are.

In 2001, Fred decided it was time to end *Mister Rogers' Neighborhood*. The final show aired on August 31, 2001. People around world were very sad. It was the longest-running children's television program in history. Fred was awarded the Presidential Medal of Freedom for the work he did for children. Fred had a special, gentle way of talking to children. He would bend down to their level, look them right in the eye, and speak to them honestly.

> When I was a boy and I would see scary things in the news, my mother would say to me, 'Look for the helpers. You will always find people who are helping.'

Fred spent his final years with his family. Sadly, in 2003, not long after he retired, he got sick and passed away. Fred left a **legacy**, or made a difference, long after he was gone. He won more than 200 other awards and was given more than 40 **honorary degrees** from **universities**. He was a role model in the lives of millions of children, many of whom are now parents and teachers.

His message is still alive today. Fred Rogers Productions makes children's TV shows like *Daniel Tiger's Neighborhood, Odd Squad,* and

JUMP
—IN THE—
THINK TANK

How can people live on long after they are gone? Is it their love, their life's work, or their memory that stays alive?

Through the Woods. The creators of other well-known children's shows like *Blue's Clues* and *Wonder Pets!* say that Mister Rogers inspired them greatly. As Mister Rogers always said, "It's such a good feeling to know that we're lifelong friends."

WHEN?

1999	2001	2002	2003
Fred gets inducted into the TV Hall of Fame.	Fred ends *Mister Rogers' Neighborhood.*	Fred earns the Presidential Medal of Freedom.	Fred Rogers dies.

CHAPTER 8

SO ... WHO WAS
FRED ROGERS
?

Challenge Accepted!

Now that you know so much about Fred's life and work, let's test your new knowledge in a little who, what, when, where, why, and how quiz. Feel free to look back in the text to find the answers if you need to, but try to remember first.

1 **Where was Fred born?**

→ A   New York, New York

→ B   Toronto, Canada

→ C   Latrobe, Pennsylvania

→ D   Winter Park, Florida

2 **How old was Fred when his baby sister, Laney, was adopted?**

→ A   11

→ B   7

→ C   3

→ D   18

3 **What were some of the puppets named on *Mister Rogers' Neighborhood*?**

→ A   Elmo, Big Bird, Mr. Snuffleupagus, Ernie

→ B   Mickey, Minnie, Goofy, Donald

→ C   Ariel, Jasmine, Belle, Cinderella

→ D   Daniel Striped Tiger, King Friday XIII, Queen Sara Saturday, X the Owl

4 **How long was *Mister Rogers' Neighborhood* on the air?**

→ A   10 years

→ B   more than 30 years

→ C   25 years

→ D   50 years

5 **Which job did Fred originally want to have?**

→ A   a baseball player

→ B   a piano player

→ C   a minister

→ D   a doctor

6 **Where did Joanne and Fred meet?**

→ A   in New York

→ B   in Pennsylvania

→ C   at Rollins College

→ D   at Dartmouth College

7 **Who had the biggest influence on Fred's life?**

→ A   his grandpa McFeely

→ B   his high school English teacher

→ C   his friends

→ D   Paul, the boy he spent a summer with

8 **In which cities did Fred and his wife live?**

→ A   San Francisco, Paris, and London

→ B   New York, Toronto, and Pittsburgh

→ C   Detroit, Chicago, and Barcelona

→ D   Dublin, Los Angeles, and Phoenix

9 What serious topics did Fred talk about on his show?

→ A clowns, cars, and cats

→ B feelings, death, and divorce

→ C snakes, salamanders, and swimming pools

→ D how to knit a sweater

10 In what year did the show end?

→ A 2020

→ B 1999

→ C 1967

→ D 2001

 **Our World**

Fred Rogers made a huge difference in the lives of millions of children who are now adults. Let's take a look at some of the ways he influenced our world for the better:

→ Teachers, parents, and children became less afraid to discuss important topics and talk through emotions. Social-emotional learning, circle time, and class meetings all mimic, or take after, the idea that Fred had for kids to talk about their feelings in order to work through them.

→ Other children's TV shows, like *Blue's Clues*, took after *Mister Rogers' Neighborhood* by mixing puppets, music, and song and teaching messages like kindness, cooperation, and how to lend a helping hand in tough times.

→ Many children who lived in homes with hard things going on tuned in to his show and heard the clear message that they were special and lovable just as they are. Sometimes, nobody else but Mister Rogers told them that in their life. Their children now watch *Daniel Tiger's Neighborhood*.

JUMP
—IN THE—
THINK TANK
FOR

⁓ MORE! ⁓

Now let's think a little more about what Fred did and how his show affected the world we currently live in.

→ How did Fred's willingness to talk about tough topics help parents support their children and make it easier for kids to deal with their emotions?

→ How did the puppets in the Neighborhood of Make-Believe allow kids to listen and understand in a way they might not have if a teacher or parent were telling them the same things?

→ What did it mean to the world when Fred went to Washington, DC, to ask the government to keep giving money to PBS?

Glossary

advice: A suggestion of the best way of doing something

audience: A group of people watching or listening to a public event

character: Someone who acts like someone else in a TV show, a movie, or a play onstage

child development: The study of changes in the body, brain, language, thoughts, and emotions of a child between birth and adulthood

civil rights movement: A time of struggle during the 1950s and 1960s when Black people in the United States fought to end racial discrimination and have equal rights

community: A group of people living near each other and/or sharing similar attitudes, interests, and goals

confidence: Believing and trusting in yourself as capable, lovable, and worthy

Congress: Part of the US government that makes laws, made up of representatives from different parts of the country

decade: A period of 10 years

direct: To manage the actors in a movie or TV show

divorce: The legal end of a marriage between two people

economy: The resources and wealth of a country or place, especially the making, selling, and using of goods and services

educational: Meant to teach something to someone else

equality: When every person has the same rights and opportunities

generation: A group of people growing up in the same time period

generous: Showing kindness by giving something, such as money or time, to another person or group

Great Depression: A period of time in history during which people had little money to spend, work was scarce, and many businesses failed. It lasted from 1929 until the 1930s and affected countries all over the world.

honorary degree: An academic degree that a school or university awards because of something special a person has done for the nation or world, instead of taking classes and tests at the school

illegal: Against the law

induct: To admit someone formally to a group or organization, like a hall of fame

legacy: Something a person leaves behind for which they are remembered

manager: A person who is in control of the activities of a show or in a company

Martin Luther King Jr.: An American minister and activist who led the civil rights movement from 1955 until he was killed in 1968

mentor: An experienced and trusted adviser who helps teach you how to do something you've never done before but that they are good at

musician: A person who plays musical instruments or is musically talented

Navy: A branch of the armed forces that carries out military operations mostly at sea

ordained minister: A person who can oversee ceremonies in the church such as baptisms, weddings, and funerals

pastor: Someone who leads a church and is ordained, or selected, to be in charge

preacher: Someone who speaks, or gives sermons, about the Bible or religion

producer: A person who pays for and/or manages the making of a movie, play, or TV show

psychologist: An expert in human behavior and the brain who helps people by listening to them talk about their problems

puppetry: The art of moving puppets, either by strings from above or by placing your hand inside the puppet, and speaking as if you are its voice

religious: Believing in a religion and practicing it often

segregation: The separation, by law, of different racial groups in a country, community, or business

Space Shuttle *Challenger*: A space shuttle that broke apart just over a minute after takeoff on January 28, 1986, killing all seven crew members on board

studio crew: Camera people, floor managers, and assistants responsible for assisting the making of a TV show

technology: Machinery and equipment made by using scientific knowledge

TV station: A business that broadcasts shows through a television

unconditionally: Without any conditions, no matter what

universities: Colleges and schools for higher learning where students earn advanced degrees

viewers: People who watch a TV show or movie

wealthy: Very rich or having a lot of money

Bibliography

A Beautiful Day in the Neighborhood. Directed by Marielle Heller. Los Angeles: Sony Pictures, 2019.

Encyclopaedia Britannica. "Fred Rogers: American Television Personality." Accessed on March 25, 2020. Britannica.com/biography/fred-rogers.

King, Maxwell. *The Good Neighbor: The Life and Work of Fred Rogers.* New York: Abrams Press, 2018.

MisterRogers.org. Accessed March 25, 2020.

Mister Rogers and Me. Directed by Benjamin Wagner. Arlington, VA: PBS, 2012.

Mister Rogers' Neighborhood: Episodes 1–912. Created by Fred Rogers. Pittsburgh: PBS, 1967–2001.

Rogers, Fred. *A Beautiful Day in the Neighborhood: Neighborly Words of Wisdom from Mister Rogers.* New York: Penguin Books, 1994.

Won't You Be My Neighbor? Directed by Morgan Neville. Los Angeles: Focus Films, 2018.

Acknowledgments

First and foremost, I want to thank Fred Rogers for being such a steady, calm influence in my life as a child. I watched *Mister Rogers' Neighborhood* daily and hung on his every word. He was a beacon of positivity and kindness in my little world. I appreciate my outstanding editor, Orli, who entrusted me with this book and guided me with grace, precision, and determination. I appreciate my parents, Janice and Ray, for their encouragement. To my brother, Steve, thanks! Kudos to my talented writers' group—Andrew, Brandi, Evan, Kyle, and Sonia. In memory of my grandma Grace, my aunt Judy, and my mentor, Ilse. To my nephews Sam, Jacob, and David, and my nieces, Sofia and Katherine. Thanks to the entire Callisto team! I am supported by family and friends: Michelle G., Susan, Ann and Greg, Danielle, Jeanne, Deborah, Kiernan, Laurie, Tanya, Carla, Julia and Ira, Maureen, Amparo, Michael, Ricardo, Alejandra, Arden, Jen, Tami, Karen, Annie, Crystal, Bryan, Jessica, Marji, Marcy, Lara, Anita and Bob, Jerry, Nena and Mel, Jami, Stacy and Rick, Laura and Darren, Michelle R., Chalmers, Violeta, Diana y Juanca, and Sylvia Boorstein.

—SBK

About the Author

Susan B. Katz is an award-winning bilingual author, National Board Certified Teacher, educational consultant, and keynote speaker. She taught for more than 25 years. Susan has published 10 books with Scholastic, Random House, Rockridge Press, and Barefoot Books. *Meditation Station*, a book about trains and mindfulness, is due out in fall 2020 with Bala Books (Shambhala) and won the International Book Award for Children's Mind/Body/Spirit. Her other titles include *ABC, Baby Me!*, *My Mama Earth* (Moonbeam Gold Award winner for best picture book and named a "top green toy" by Education.com), *ABC School's for Me* (illustrated by Lynn Munsinger, and *All Year Round,* which she translated into Spanish as *Un Año Redondo* for Scholastic. She also authored *The Story of Ruth Bader Ginsburg, The Story of Frida Kahlo, The Story of Jane Goodall, The Story of Albert Einstein,* and *The Story of Marie Curie* for Rockridge Press. Susan is also the executive director of ConnectingAuthors.org, a national nonprofit bringing children's book authors and illustrators into schools. She served as the strategic partner manager for authors at Facebook. When she's not writing, Susan enjoys traveling, salsa dancing, and spending time at the beach. You can find out more about her books and school visits at **SusanKatzBooks.com**.

About the Illustrator

Can Tuğrul is an illustrator of children's books / collector of old medals / protector of street cats / traveler of flea markets / passenger of night trains / owner of the last cookies / addict of postcards / watcher of sci-fi movies / lover of long journeys. Can currently lives in Istanbul and is always drawing something.

WHO WILL INSPIRE YOU NEXT?

EXPLORE A WORLD OF HEROES AND ROLE MODELS IN
THE STORY OF ...BIOGRAPHY SERIES FOR NEW READERS.

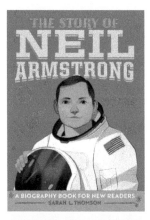
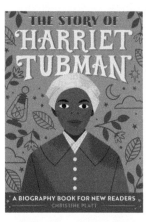
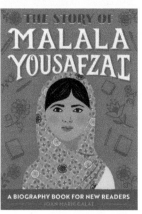

LOOK FOR THIS SERIES
WHEREVER BOOKS AND EBOOKS ARE SOLD

Alexander Hamilton	Jane Goodall
Albert Einstein	Barack Obama
Martin Luther King Jr.	Helen Keller
George Washington	Marie Curie